Old Rosemount
Patricia Newman

The Victoria Park fountain is a Category A listed structure built of granite from fourteen local quarries and designed by John Bridgeford Pirie who was born in Aberdeen in 1848, the son of a sea captain. The fountain was presented to the people of the city in 1881 by the Granite Polishers and Builders of Aberdeen. It was estimated to have cost £500. The outer basin is 45 feet in diameter with further basins above it reducing in size and the uppermost tiers made of copper. The fountain still graces the centre of the park although it is no longer a water feature. Hopefully, this will be rectified so that future Aberdonians can enjoy the fountain as it should be.

468 The Wallace Statue, Aberdeen
Guardians of Scotland, Past and Present
Adelphi Series

Text © Patricia Newman, 2015
First published in the United Kingdom, 2015,
by Stenlake Publishing Ltd.
www.stenlake.co.uk
ISBN 978-1-84033-719-8

The publishers regret that they cannot supply
copies of any pictures featured in this book.

Printed by
P2D Books, 1 Newlands Rd, Westoning, Bedford, MK45 5LD

Acknowledgements

David Main and David Oswald, Library and Information Services, Aberdeen City Council for permission to use photographs from their collection
Eleanore McKay and Brian Watt for permission to use postcards
Allan Condie for postcards and for invaluable information on trams
Ian Haw for the photograph of Bonnymuir Bowling Club
Rosie and Ian Nicol for their generous help and encouragement
Jen Dalmain for help identifying locations
Graeme Milne for help with research
And to my proof reader for all his help.

The inscription reads "*I tell you a truth, liberty is the best of all things, my son, never live under any slavish bond.*" The massive bronze statue of Sir William Wallace, sculpted by William Grant Stevenson and funded by a legacy for the purpose by John Steill, stands opposite His Majesty's Theatre on Rosemount Viaduct. The legacy was in excess of £3,000. The Duthie Park was originally proposed as a site for the statue but the viaduct was chosen by the Trustees of Mr. Steill. The pedestal was constructed of pink Correnie granite by the Aberdeen firm of John Morgan.

Introduction

The lands known as the Forest of Stocket were granted to the people of Aberdeen by King Robert the Bruce in gratitude for their support in his battles for the crown of Scotland. The area covered was roughly six miles by four. This was of huge benefit to Aberdeen as tenants afterwards paid their rents to Aberdeen instead of to the Crown. The Freedom Lands and the rents from them formed the source of the Common Good Fund.

Over the years, some land has been added to the Freedom Lands. However, in times of hardship, Aberdeen had to sell off some of the land thus depleting the resource. The Common Good Fund still exists today and is used for the benefit of the city as a whole.

This book contains 19th and 20th century photographs of some of the streets, buildings and parks within the areas originally covered by the Forest of Stocket and adjacent streets.

Until the great work of extending Aberdeen in the first decade of the 19th century, Aberdeen was an over crowded medieval city bounded by the natural landscape. The sea to the east, the Rivers Dee and Don to the north and south and, the valley of the Denburn to the west kept Aberdeen contained. Access to the north was by way of Old Aberdeen to the Brig of Balgownie over the River Don. This was the only local bridge to the north until 1827.

Until the Municipality Extension Act of 1871, Rosemount was outwith the City of Aberdeen and was largely open fields, farmhouses and a few isolated houses. One of these houses was Rosemount after which the area was named.

In 1800, as the result of the New Streets Act, a huge engineering work was undertaken to drive west from the city into the area beyond the Denburn. St. Katherine's Hill was reduced in height, Union Street was created on a series of concealed arches and the Denburn was crossed by Union Bridge. The cost of this monumental work temporarily bankrupted the city and it was some time before the full benefit of the additional space for housing was realised.

By the 1880s, the ever-expanding city looked to the Rosemount area to provide housing for the workers flocking to the newly industrialised city. A design by the engineer, William Boulton, was chosen to span the Denburn twice in one skewed viaduct. This design provided a smooth transition from the city to the spine of Rosemount.

Rosemount House was built prior to 1810. In 1836 it was advertised to let and was described as being "commodious and well finished and having a pleasant view of the town and bay". There is no longer a view of the town or the bay as the house is completely surrounded by later buildings. In 1883 the council bought 85 square yards of the garden in front of Rosemount House to build tenements on the line of Rosemount Place. An area was retained to form a pend giving access to Rosemount House. Mr. Smith, the owner of Rosemount Place, was paid £38 compensation.

Looking east from Rosemount Viaduct to School Hill, the Denburn Viaduct leads to the older part of Aberdeen. The Triple Kirks (on the right of the photograph) were built to house three Disruption congregations – the East, West and South parishes. The Disruption came about in 1843 when members and 450 clergy of the (established) Church of Scotland decided to leave and form the Free Church of Scotland in order to have freedom of jurisdiction over spiritual matters. The dispute came to a head over the right of patronage whereby wealthy landowners could impose a minister of their choice on a congregation. The building was designed by Archibald Simpson and was the only church in Scotland built to house three congregations. It is also unusual as it was built of brick whereas the majority of central Aberdeen is built of granite. The dome of what was the Central School – now a shopping centre - can be seen in the centre of the photograph.

The Denburn Viaduct has three arches to span the valley of the Denburn and provide access for the Denburn Railway running from Waterloo Goods Station to Kittybrewster where it joined the line north to Keith in what is now Morayshire. Schoolhill Railway Station below the viaduct was built in 1889. In order to get to the lower level, a strange pedestrian bridge was built to join the pavement on the viaduct to a rectangular three storey building, visible behind the bus. Passengers entered the building at second storey level and descended through it to the station below. When the station closed, the top floor became a café. The building was demolished in the 1970s. Viscount Cowdray and his wife, Annie, funded the Cowdray Hall – right of the photograph – "with a view to encouraging the taste for art and music in the City of Aberdeen". Sir Weetman Cowdray was a British engineer and industrialist who lived at Dunecht House. Designed by Alexander Marshall Mackenzie in 1885 and constructed of Rubislaw, Kemnay and Correnie granite, the hall provides a venue for the arts. Lunchtime concerts are held there and once upon a time, generations of Aberdonians learned ballroom dancing with Madame Murray. The pillared war memorial in the centre of the photograph was built by public subscription in 1920 and remembers the dead of two World Wars. It was designed by A. Marshall Mackenzie and Son. The lion sculpture was designed by William MacMillan, A.R.A. Created from massive blocks of Kemnay granite in 1925, it was carved by James Philip and George Cooper in Arthur Taylor's Jute Street works.

On the right of the photograph is the series of buildings known to Aberdonians as Education, Salvation and Damnation. Looking west to Rosemount Viaduct, the building with the two drum ventilators on the roof – centre right of the photograph is the Central Library – Education. The Aberdeen Free Library, as it was originally known, was built on a corner site between Rosemount Viaduct and Lower Skene Street. The cost of construction (£10,000) was met by public subscription aided by a generous donation of £2,000 by Mr. and Mrs. Andrew Carnegie who opened the building in 1892. It is now a Category C listed building. The building next to it with the impressive dome is St. Mark's Church – Salvation. It was built to house the South Parish congregation when it moved from the Triple Kirks. St. Mark's was designed by A Marshall Mackenzie and is surmounted by a dome that is said to be modelled on St. Paul's in London. In 1972 the building was renamed St. Mark's and became home to the East and Belmont churches. In 1981 Trinity Church also found a home at St. Mark's. The building on the near right is His Majesty's Theatre – Damnation. The site was purchased for £230 by the Arthur Theatre Company from Aberdeen City Council. It was designed by Frank Matcham, the famous English theatre architect who was also responsible for the Hackney Empire and the London Palladium. Built in the first decade of the twentieth century, it was named after King Edward VII. The auditorium is a magnificent example of Edwardian style. At around the same time, Her Majesty's Theatre on Guild Street was revamped, also by Matcham, and renamed The Tivoli. The first production to be staged was "Little Red Riding Hood" on December 3rd 1906. Seats were priced at 4, 3 and 2 shillings.

St. Columba Free Church is on the right of the photograph on Rosemount Viaduct. The foundation stone was laid in 1895 and the church was designed by the architect Alexander Ellis of Ellis and Wilson. The building cost £6,523, most of which was funded by the sale of the congregation's former church on Union Terrace. It provides an imposing culmination to the fine terrace of tenements on Rosemount Viaduct – also designed by Ellis and Wilson. The No. 6 tram travelled on the clockwise circuit of the Rosemount route. This tram is 132 and was one of the Brush Engineering models purchased in 1929. The Northern Co-operative Society's grocer shop can be seen on the lower left of the photograph at the corner of Baker Street. This is still a food store but under different ownership. The street on the right of the photograph was part of Stevenson Street according to the Plan of the City of Aberdeen of 1915. It turned through ninety degrees when it reached the side wall of the church and continued down to Upper Denburn. Modern flats now occupy this site with a stairway down to Stevenson Street along the side of the church.

In 1739 the Town Council decided that Aberdeen required a workhouse and an infirmary. The infirmary was to care for the sick poor who were "honest and laborious". The Council decided on a site west of the town where there was good air that would benefit the sick. The workhouse was to be situated near the Tolbooth in the centre of Aberdeen. Accordingly, a house was built and staff employed to care for the sick. The original building was quite small, with space for only around six or seven patients. In 1745/6, the infirmary was occupied by wounded soldiers of one side or the other in the '45 rebellion. Thereafter, the infirmary was gradually enlarged as the need for beds grew until it could accommodate 80 patients. A Royal Charter was granted in 1773 resulting in a change of name to Aberdeen Royal Infirmary. In Alexander Milne's map of 1789, the infirmary is shown as an 'H' shaped building or series of buildings.

The Wards, Royal Infirmary, Aberdeen

By 1832 it was agreed that the hospital needed to expand again and, as a first step, fever wards were constructed at some distance from the main building to the north of the site. In 1840 Archibald Simpson's grand new infirmary, as seen opposite, had been built on the same site at a cost of £16,700. In 1886 further expansion was carried out retaining Simpson's building for administration offices but creating wards and surgical theatres as seen in the photograph above. However, by the 20th century, further expansion was required and would not be possible in the already cramped site at Woolmanhill. In 1929, the city was reported to have raised nearly half a million pounds to build a new hospital at Foresterhill.

Rosemount Viaduct leads into South Mount Street and thence to its junction with South Mount Street. This photograph shows the No. 3 tram negotiating the bend into Rosemount Place. The No. 3 tram travelled anti-clockwise on the Rosemount Circle line. The bank at the corner is the Clydesdale and North of Scotland Bank. The Clydesdale Bank was started in 1838 in Glasgow. It became an associate of the London City and Midland Bank (later known just as the Midland Bank) in 1920. The Midland Bank bought the North of Scotland Bank in 1923 and the two Scottish banks were amalgamated in 1950 becoming the Clydesdale and North of Scotland Bank. After a time, the bank's name was shortened to the Clydesdale Bank. The tenement above the bank and the one adjacent to it have nepus gables – a particularly Scottish architectural feature. Nepus gables are small gables on the front of the building carrying the chimney stacks and often with windows as can be seen in these examples.

The Aberdeen Municipality Extension Act of 1873 took the Rosemount area into the city and allowed expansion of city housing. From then on, houses began to be built but access was difficult until Rosemount Viaduct was constructed. Tenement housing was built along Rosemount Place and some adjacent streets to house families of men with steady work. The poor and those with only intermittent work were left in the overcrowded slums. Shops were provided on the ground floor of many of the tenement blocks along Rosemount Place especially at its corners with side streets. Hill Street was and is a small street off Rosemount Place. It is a street of Victorian tenements built in the early 1880s on the site of the former House of Refuge and School of Industry for Boys. At the end of Hill Street, between it and Farner's Hall Lane stood Rosemount Works, a factory making tape and winceys – a plain wool and cotton fabric. At the corner stood the traditional grocer's shop serving the local community long before supermarkets. This photograph was probably taken in the 1940s when Rosemount Place still had granite setts or cassies instead of tarmac as it is today. Of course, there was rationing and also shortages to contend with in the 1940s. Wilburn Ltd had a number of grocer shops in Aberdeen from the 1930s to the 1950s but this was the smallest. However, it carried a large range of groceries – fresh fruit and veg, bread, biscuits and cakes from their bakery in Rennies Wynd, tinned goods and dairy produce. Shops in Aberdeen at that time had a half day on Wednesday. There was no Sunday trading and shops were open until 7 or 8pm with assistants often working a 65 hour week. In 1934 shop workers were demanding a 5% rise in wages to the equivalent of £3 3s per week and a reduction in working hours to 40 per week, giving an hourly rate of approximately 1s 7d. Tea arrived in the shop in wooden tea chests and sugar in hundredweight bags. Both had to be weighed out and packaged. Potatoes were sold loose as were biscuits which were on display in tins with clear lids. The photograph shows the staff in their white aprons. Leslie Morrison, on the left, was the manager and later the owner of the shop. Grocers served a seven year apprenticeship usually after a year as a message boy.

Typically for the time, the Rosemount tenements were three or four storeys high with toilets on the half landings or in the lobby on the ground floor. On the right of the photogrpah is Rutherford Free Church and Hall. This Free Presbyterian church was built in 1863 when the membership of the then rural community was 203. However, with the expansion of the city, by 1900 membership stood at 878. The church was designed by Henderson and Sons of Loch Street and the first service was held on Feb 9th 1870. It was named after Samuel Rutherford, who lived in the 17th century and was an ardent non-conformist. It is a Category C listed building. The building is now flats, and offices.Beyond the church, at the entrance to Loanhead Terrace, stands Loanhead Cottage where the Queen Vic public house stands today. On the left is the Northern Co-operative Society's tenement with shops below. The main area was the grocery department with the butter on the right and dry goods on the left. The flats above the shops were occupied by staff in the early days. In 1895 there were no numbers in Rosemount Place higher than 137 on the left and 142 on the right. By 1900 numbers 182 to 286 were also present, so lots of building in just five years! The first street on the left is Short Loanings (short lane) where the Co-op built more shops and tenements. This street leads to Leadside Road. The second street on the left is Esslemont Avenue.

Thomson Street was named after James Thomson, a house carpenter and a member of the Incorporated Trades. The street was built by the mason, John Morgan, who was born at Craigton Farm, Kennethmont, the son of a farmer. He built and lived in 57 Thomson Street, calling the house Monte Rosa, until he moved to 50 Queen's Road. In 1881 his building firm employed 80 men. Monte Rosa Cottage (no. 57) is a Listed Building. Air raid shelters were common all over Aberdeen during and just after the Second World War and one survives in the back garden of the flats at 40 Thomson Street.

This terrace was laid out by the Wrights and Coopers Incorporation. In an Ordnance Survey map of 1867, Rosemount Place went from Skene Square to Short Loanings. Further west, the name changed to Loanhead. Thus Loanhead Terrace was a logical name for the new street. It was not until the map of 1912 that the name Rosemount Place was adopted for the whole length. Loanhead Terrace can be justly proud of one of its early sons, Lieutenant Archibald Bisset Smith. He was born in Cults and later lived with his parents at 65 Loanhead Terrace. After studying at Robert Gordon's College, he served in the Merchant Navy commanding New Zealand merchant ships. In 1917, Smith was master of the New Zealand Shipping Company's steamer SS *Otaki*, a refrigerated vessel sailing under ballast from London to New York. She was attacked by the German ship *Moewe*. A fierce running battle ensued despite *Otaki* having only one 4.7 inch gun while the converted freighter, *Moewe*, had seven guns and two torpedo tubes. The *Moewe* was pitching in the rough seas while the *Otaki*, being heavier was a steady platform for her one gun. However, at length, the *Otaki* began taking on water and Smith gave the order to take to the boats. He remained on board and went down with his ship. After the war, Smith was given an ante-dated commission in the Royal Navy Voluntary Reserve and awarded the Victoria Cross. In 1936, Smith's family gave Robert Gordon's College the Otaki Shield to be awarded to an outstanding pupil each year. Another notable son of Loanhead Terrace was George Milne Fraser who lived for a time at No. 16. He is remembered as an historian, librarian and author. Born in Methlick in 1862, his family moved to Aberdeen to find work, living in Minister Lane. Young George initially worked as a stonecutter but lost an eye in an accident. Subsequently he worked as a journalist and then, despite the lack of an academic background, became the City Librarian, a post he held for nearly 40 years. During this time, he wrote books on local history and current writers are indebted to him for this.

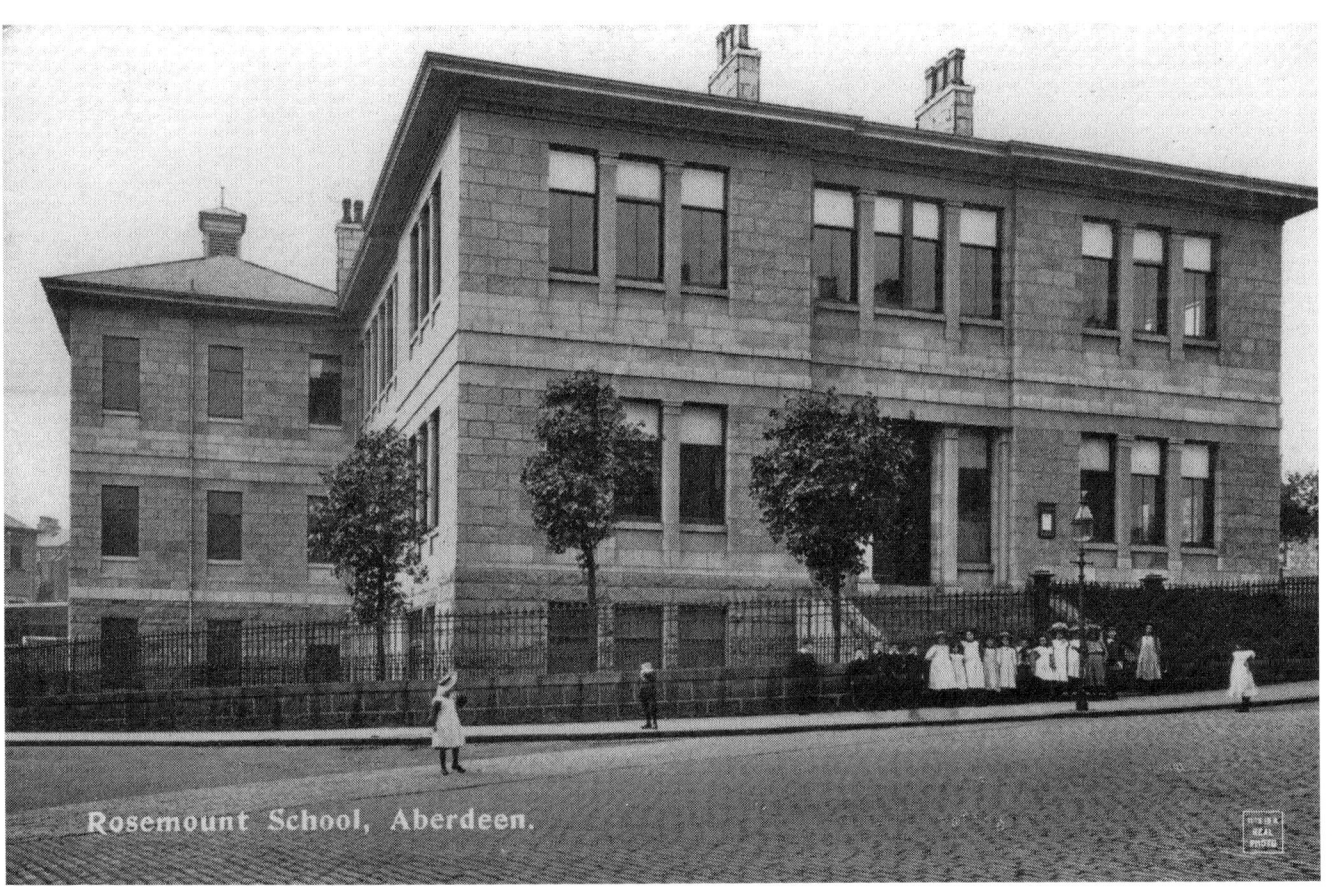

Rosemount School, Aberdeen.

This school stands at the junction of Esslemont Avenue and Rosemount Place. It was built in 1883-4 to a design by James Souttar. The cost of construction was £8,000 and the Town Council voted to pay Mr. Souttar £50 when the work was completed to their satisfaction. The *Aberdeen Evening Express* noted that the temperature in the school could be maintained at 55°F – just under 13°C! A little chilly for today's youngsters, but at the time the school was built children were accustomed to cold homes and wore warmer clothes. In 1897, a proposal to extend the school upwards by the addition of a fourth floor was vetoed and Westfield School (incorporating Chalmers Girls School) was constructed to fill the need for more space. Chalmers School had been purchased from the heritors in 1899. The Town Council had lost a legal battle against the School Board whereby they argued that the Grammar School policies could only be used for higher education and not elementary. By 1901 Rosemount School was again overcrowded so it was extended onto adjacent land and some remodelling of the interior was carried out. During the First World War, the school was turned into a military hospital to house the wounded – part of the 1st Scottish General Hospital. This meant that Rosemount children had to share premises with Mile End School with pupils from each school attending half a day. Mile End children started classes at 8.30am, finishing at 1pm. Rosemount pupils started at 1.30pm and finished at 6pm. Just round the corner, in Belgrave Terrace, lived Miss Mary Garden the opera soprano. Miss Garden was more famous abroad than she was at home. She travelled widely in Europe and the USA, singing in many famous opera houses and was the leading singer in the Opéra-Comique in Paris. For more than 20 years, she lived and worked in Chicago, as Managing Director of Chicago Opera. She retired to her home in Aberdeen in 1949.

In the latter half of the 19th century and the beginning of the 20th the Rosemount area grew with tenements, shops and private housing being built. This is the junction of Rosemount Place with Watson Street on the right. The shop at 1 Watson Street was at one time a wine and spirit shop but by the 1950s, was a newsagent run by the famous Aberdeen and Scotland footballer "gentleman" George Hamilton. Watson Street was laid out in 1864 long before the tenements on the right were built in 1898 and had shops on the ground floor. In the 1950s there was the Balgownie Dairy - Miss Murison, the confectioners - Sandy Warrender (in his brown shop coat) and another newsagent - Alex Lindsay. Above the shops were tenement flats with toilets on the half landing and there was coal in the basement cellars a long way to carry coal up the stairs before a fire could be lit.

Watson Street was built of ground owned by the Shoemakers' Incorporation – one of the Seven Incorporated Trades. It was named after the then Deacon of the Craft, Baillie George Watson who owned the land on which the street was built. Baillie Watson, who died at the age of 75 in 1863, had his shoemaker's shop in the Netherkirkgate and was known for hard work both at his trade and for charity. The street runs from Westburn Road to Rosemount Place with Victoria Park to the right. On valuation roll for 1895 Watson Street was quite complete, with Nos. 1 to 63 and 2 to 64 listed. William Alexander (1826-1894) lived at 19 Watson Street for several years in the 1870s. He was editor of the *Aberdeen Free Press* and author of *Johnny Gibb of Gushetneuk*. He was fluent in the Doric having been born and raised in Chapel of Garioch. Later, he moved to Belvidere Street.

Belvidere Crescent runs from Rosemount Place to Hamilton Place at Craigie Loanings. It was named after a house of the same name in the area occupied by John Ewing of Shelagreen, an advocate in Aberdeen. The Crescent was built in the early 1890s by various builders. However, despite this they nevertheless have a uniform appearance. Duncan McMillan was the architect of a number of the houses in the Crescent and also of some prestigious houses in Queen's Road and Rubislaw Den. Both World Wars brought tragedy to this terrace as they did to nearly every street in the town. In the First World War, Lt. John McHardy was killed leading his company at Chaudon in 1918. In the Second World War, Captain James Wyness of the Royal Artillery and son of Captain and Mrs. Wyness died of wounds in 1944. He had been awarded the Military Cross for conspicuous gallantry in 1943. His brother William died while serving in the Merchant Navy in 1942.

Originally, Belvidere Street extended north to what is now Westburn Road. However, in 1872, when the land known as Glennie's Parks was purchased to create the Victoria Park, the Council decided to make Belvidere Street a cul-de-sac. At the same time a new road, Loanhead Place, was created to link Thomson Street to Watson Street. The photograph was taken looking north from Rosemount Place; Victoria Park and its fountain can be seen in the distance. The house on the right of the photograph is 250 Rosemount Place, a late 19th century semi-detached cottage with a Grade C Listing. Although there are no listed buildings in Belvidere Street, it is within the Rosemount and Westburn Conservation Area. On the left is a stepped terrace of granite houses with front gardens and railings. The second house on the left is No. 3, the final home of William Alexander, newspaper editor and author. The house was named Gushetneuk after his novel, *Johnny Gibb of Gushetneuk*. It has a memorial plaque on the wall.

Victoria Park was built on land called Glennie's Park (park meaning field in this instance). It was opened to the public in 1871. It had cost the Common Good Fund in the region of £4,000 to convert cold, wet pasture into a park to be enjoyed by the people of Rosemount. Originally, the park had only a few ash trees but over the following twelve years, a wide variety of species were planted such as poplars, limes, willows and maple. There is a wonderful granite fountain in the centre of the park. In the early years, according to the local press, there were goldfish and trout in the lower tier of the fountain and a large eel lived in the upper basin. Today the garden offers a tranquil oasis in the middle of bustling Rosemount. It has peaceful tree-lined walks, beautiful shrubs and a sensory garden.

The lodge is a Category C listed building. Robert Walker was keeper of the park from the beginning and was awarded an increase in salary from £65 to £188 in 1878 in recognition of his work there and at other planted areas in the city. He was Parks and Gardens Superintendent from 1872 to his retirement in 1919, living in the Lodge. Robert had trained at Roy's Nursery in Ferryhill. In 1914, he was promoted to the position of General Superintendent of all the city parks at an annual salary of £200 and added Duthie and Walker Parks to his work in Westburn, Victoria and Stewart Parks as well as the planting at the Links. He also had responsibility for Union Terrace Gardens, as the planting developed there. The cold frames and greenhouses of Victoria Park provided bedding plants for the Victoria and Westburn parks. Robert Walker was also instrumental in planting a garden at Sunnybank School so that the children could learn about cultivation.

Westburn Road, Aberdeen.

Westburn Road is a continuation of Hutcheon Street and runs westwards until it joins the Lang Stracht, passing Aberdeen Royal Infirmary (Foresterhill Hospital). Formerly, it had several names along its length – Ann Place, Mary Place and Mount Place. The Royal Cornhill Hospital is a psychiatric hospital nearer to Aberdeen than in this photograph. It was founded in 1800 on the Clerkseat Estate as the Aberdeen Lunatic Asylum. The original asylum building was designed by Archibald Simpson in 1819 and completed by John Smith, another notable architect from Aberdeen. 32 Westburn Road is the former lodge to Cornhill Hospital and a listed building, designed by William Ramage. This is now lost behind a wall in the hospital grounds. Its only purpose seems to be to indicate the site of the original entrance. The cottages on the right are no longer and the Clan Cancer support centre is now on this land.

In the 1920s, Professor Matthew Hay, Aberdeen's City Medical Officer of Health since 1888, suggested that a large site to accommodate the various hospitals in one place would be beneficial for the city. This resulted in the formation of the Joint Hospitals scheme. Although the scheme met with many setbacks, Professor Hay was successful in his plans. Foresterhill on the outskirts of Aberdeen provided space for a general hospital as well as maternity and children's hospitals. Professor Hay had pointed out the location to his son 20 years before the Joint Hospital scheme was developed. He wanted a big open space high above the huddled city. In addition to the general hospital, there was a nurses' home and Aberdeen University's Medical School. This unification of medical services in one area was the first of its kind although it is now the norm. Indeed, it is now considered to be the largest hospital complex in Europe. The hospital was renamed the Aberdeen Royal Infirmary and the infirmary of that name in the centre of town became Woolmanhill. The original hospital building was designed by James Brown Nicol in 1927 and the foundation stone was laid in 1928. The hospital opened in 1936. However, it would be some years before services such as Accident and Emergency would be accommodated at Foresterhill.

Westburn Park was named after Westburn House which in turn was named after the West Burn of Gilcomston which runs through the park. In the distance, to the left of the photograph, the Doric portico of Westburn House can be seen. Although only Westburn Road separates them, Westburn Park has a very different atmosphere from Victoria Park as it has no flower beds and is mainly grass with magnificent mature trees and wide open spaces for children to play as well as pitches laid out for various sports. It is approximately 24 acres in extent. Originally the park was fenced and gated to prevent animals straying onto the grass. The park is on the site of the small estate of Westburn. It was purchased from the then owner, David Chalmers and was opened to the public on 7th May 1901. Robert Walker of Victoria Park was instrumental in planning the park and its trees. These included Lombardy poplars imported from Hamburg. They were planted in 1906 at the eastern end of the park and provided a contrast with the purple plane trees. Westburn House, designed by Archibald Simpson, was converted to refreshment rooms.

THE NEW ROYAL INFIRMARY, FORRESTERHILL, ABERDEEN
PHOTO A. J. B. STRACHAN

In the 1920s, Professor Matthew Hay, Aberdeen's City Medical Officer of Health since 1888, suggested that a large site to accommodate the various hospitals in one place would be beneficial for the city. This resulted in the formation of the Joint Hospitals scheme. Although the scheme met with many setbacks, Professor Hay was successful in his plans. Foresterhill on the outskirts of Aberdeen provided space for a general hospital as well as maternity and children's hospitals. Professor Hay had pointed out the location to his son 20 years before the Joint Hospital scheme was developed. He wanted a big open space high above the huddled city. In addition to the general hospital, there was a nurses' home and Aberdeen University's Medical School. This unification of medical services in one area was the first of its kind although it is now the norm. Indeed, it is now considered to be the largest hospital complex in Europe. The hospital was renamed the Aberdeen Royal Infirmary and the infirmary of that name in the centre of town became Woolmanhill. The original hospital building was designed by James Brown Nicol in 1927 and the foundation stone was laid in 1928. The hospital opened in 1936. However, it would be some years before services such as Accident and Emergency would be accommodated at Foresterhill.

Westburn Park was named after Westburn House which in turn was named after the West Burn of Gilcomston which runs through the park. In the distance, to the left of the photograph, the Doric portico of Westburn House can be seen. Although only Westburn Road separates them, Westburn Park has a very different atmosphere from Victoria Park as it has no flower beds and is mainly grass with magnificent mature trees and wide open spaces for children to play as well as pitches laid out for various sports. It is approximately 24 acres in extent. Originally the park was fenced and gated to prevent animals straying onto the grass. The park is on the site of the small estate of Westburn. It was purchased from the then owner, David Chalmers and was opened to the public on 7th May 1901. Robert Walker of Victoria Park was instrumental in planning the park and its trees. These included Lombardy poplars imported from Hamburg. They were planted in 1906 at the eastern end of the park and provided a contrast with the purple plane trees. Westburn House, designed by Archibald Simpson, was converted to refreshment rooms.

Lochhead House was once part of the Lochhead Hydropathic Establishment, reputedly the first hydropathic in Scotland. It was established in 1851 but by the late 1860s larger hydros at Crieff and Peebles had opened and Lochhead declined. The house was purchased in the 1890s by the sons of George Washington Wilson, the pioneering Scottish photographer. Charles, Louis and John Hay Wilson used the building as a lantern slide factory. They employed 40 people and were at the time one of the world's largest suppliers of photographic prints. In 1932 Lochhead House was demolished and the eastern side of Westburn Park was established on the site and grounds.

At the top of Rosemount Place, there is a junction where Mid Stocket Road branches to the right and Beechgrove Terrace (formerly South Stocket Road) to the left. The photograph shows the clockwise and anticlockwise tram tracks of the Rosemount Circle Line. The property at the junction is 1 Mid Stocket Road and has a date stone reading 1895. For many years it was a grocer's shop. It was built in the grounds of Mile End House. The house was built around 1825, and in 1882 it was put up for sale at an estimate of £2,000. The grounds were described as suitable for feuing as indeed they were having frontages on two streets.

Beechgrove Terrace runs from the top of Rosemount Place to King's Gate at its junction with Fountainhall Road. The terrace was named after Beechgrove House that was owned at one time by John Fyfe, granite merchant in the city. The Wrights and Coopers bought the house and grounds for £7,500 in 1906 with a view to feuing the land for housing. In 1936, the BBC bought Beechgrove House and the two remaining acres from T Scott Sutherland, the architect. The land became the site for the Beechgrove Garden, still a popular TV programme today. In the photograph, the No 5 tramcar is travelling from King's Gate to Castle Street. This would take it down Rosemount Place, turning right into South Mount Street, onto Rosemount Viaduct and then to Union Terrace and Union Street.

Image Courtesy of Aberdeen City Libraries

This horse bus preceded the horse trams and was run by William Bain who had been operating hackney cabs In 1862 he decided to provide horse omnibuses on some routes in Aberdeen from his depot in the old Waterhouse in Union Place – now the west end of Union Street – and also from his stables in Loch Street. However, the enterprise was fairly short-lived as they provided a very limited service. This omnibus operated on the Castle Street, Rosemount, Mile End and Rubislaw Hill route. The route used to get from Castle Street to Rosemount was probably via Skene Square as Rosemount Viaduct had not been built at that time. William Bain retired in 1921 after many years of service having seen transport move from horse buses to motor vehicles. This photograph would appear to have been taken where Beechgrove Terrace meets King's Gate.

Trams 130 and 132 negotiate the corner at the junction of Beechgrove Terrace and Fountainhall Road. On 30th November 1888, the Rosemount Circle tram line was opened. The lines operated both clockwise and anti-clockwise with the No. 3 tram travelling down Rosemount Place towards Rosemount Viaduct and the No. 6 tram travelling up Rosemount Place towards Kings Gate. The horse tram was used on the Rosemount Circle from 1888 to 1902. In December 1888, a local grocer treated the children of his customers and others in the area to a trip on the new circle line in Rosemount. Two extra cars were put on to accommodate the children. The last tram was horse-drawn by Clydesdales, Bill and Betsy on 2nd October 1954. They were more used to pulling milk carts for the Northern Co-operative Society.

This tram depot was in Fountainhall Road – formerly North St. Swithin Street. In 1874 the tram depot was opposite the one shown above and had stables for the horses that drew the tramcars. It had two entrance tracks. By 1892 the present horse-drawn tram depot had been built on the site of the old skating rink and had been adapted to take electric cars. The stables were then closed. Originally the trams were owned and run by the Aberdeen District Tramway Company but the Council took over the ownership in 1898 and electric trams were introduced. During the 24 years of private operation, 60 million passengers had been carried to and from their homes and places of work. The building ceased to be used as a tram depot in 1958. It was taken over by the BBC for a time and later demolished. Flats now occupy the site.

The view on the left of the inside of the tram depot shows three open balcony cars retained for use as salt cars. These tram cars were fitted with snow plough blades as well as carrying salt for icy tram rails. The cars had traps in the lower saloon floor to gain access to the motors and these were opened to allow the deposit of salt on the roadway. Car No. 76 was built in 1913 by the local firm of John T. Clark, coachbuilders to King George V. Their premises were in Rose Street. Originally No. 76 was built as a Pay as You Enter car but later reverted to standard with the conductor always standing on the rear platform. As 90% of accidents arose when the conductor was absent from the rear platform, the Pay as You Enter system was thought to be superior. It was also felt that at times of heavy demand, such as on a Saturday when the Dons were playing at home, the new system would ensure that everyone paid. It was estimated that the loss due to unpaid fares was 7%. Aberdeen was the first city in Europe to have this new design of car. Car No 76 was withdrawn from normal service in 1952, lasting as a salt car until the system closed in 1958.

Mile End Avenue was authorised in March 1892 to run from Mid Stocket Road to Westburn Road. It is named for Mile End House at its Mid Stocket end. Mile End House is a Category C Listed Building and in the 20th century, Dr Mary Esslemont lived there. During her lifetime, Dr Mary, as she was affectionately known, was a general practitioner in Aberdeen but her influence went far afield. She travelled all over the world as a representative of the medical profession. At home, she was an adviser on the establishment of the National Health Service and a Vice President of the British Medical Association. In 1983, she died at home aged 93. In her will, she gave Mile End House to the Soroptomist International of Aberdeen to provide housing for women over 60. The house now comprises one bedroom flats and a flat for a disabled woman and her carer.

Originally called the North Stocket Road, the name recalls the Forest of Stocket granted to the people of Aberdeen by Robert the Bruce. Loanhead House was situated to the north of the street and was the home of James Elmslie, who began the process of quarrying for granite at Loanhead Quarry nearby. Loanhead was the first quarry as we know it. Before it was opened, building stones were gathered from the surface. Loanhead furnished granite for Robert Gordon's College and for the original infirmary at Woolmanhill. Beechgrove Church of Scotland is on the left in the photograph. Founded around 1900 to serve the growing population in the area, it was designed by Brown and Watt in a Norman Gothic style. A Category B Listed Building, it was built by the Free Church of Scotland (that seceded from the Kirk at the time of the Disruption). It was built of Kemnay granite and the contractor for masonry was Alexander Anderson The congregation has now united with Saint Ninian's Church and is renamed Midstocket Church. The original Beechgrove Church building has been converted into flats. The shops on the right - 56-58 Mid Stocket Road are still thriving today. They were built between 1900 and 1905 by the Northern Co-operative Society. A Co-op baker, grocer and butcher occupied the shops and the flats above were used for storage and housing for staff. The Co-op was taking advantage of the great increase in house building in the area at that time.

Renamed Midstocket Church following its amalgamation with Beechgrove Church, St. Ninian's is situated on Mid Stocket Road between Harcourt Road and Camperdown Road. It has a seating capacity of around 800. The church was designed by William Kelly who is widely accepted as the designer of Kelly's Cats – the leopards on Union Bridge. The foundation stone was laid in October 1898 and the service of dedication was held on 5th September 1900. It was reported that there were twelve churches in Aberdeen in 1843, with a very limited attendance after the Disruption. By 1900 there were 22 churches connected with the Church of Scotland.

This view of Mid Stocket Road shows Beechgrove Church to the right and the entrance to Hosefield Avenue to the left. In 1802 the lands of Hosefield belonged to Alexander Livingston, an Aberdeen merchant who sold the land to pay off creditors of a failed enterprise but then went to Rotterdam and was a successful merchant and banker. By 1894 the land was owned by Aberdeen University who applied to the Roads Committee for permission to build a new street called Hosefield Avenue and to feu the ground on both sides for housing. The gable end of the first house in Hosefield Avenue shows a good example of 'Aberdeen Bond'. This was a type of building developed by masons in Aberdeen when cutting granite was difficult. It involved interspersing large stones with two or three smaller filler stones and then another large stone on each course. Small thin stones were sometimes used in between courses as well. This area looks very similar today with a few exceptions. The garden railings all disappeared in the Second World War, the pillar box has moved to the other corner and the street lamps are more modern.

The former Mile End Primary School is on Mid Stocket Road at its junction with Gordondale Road. Gordondale Road was named after a house in the vicinity. The school was built in 1899 at a cost of just over £12,000 to serve the increasing population of the Mid Stocket area. The architect was A H L Mackinnon. There was a "servitor's cottage" in the grounds for use of the janitorial staff. The opening of this large building allowed the Council to close Rubislaw Public School and transfer pupils to Mile End. The school along with the servitor's cottage, walls and gates and gatepiers and railings are all listed Category C. Both the school and the servitor's cottage have been approved for conversion into homes.

This photograph shows houses on the north side of Mid Stocket Road at its junction with Rosebery Street. In the distance can be seen the tower of the former St. Ninians Church, now Midstocket Church. The houses in Rosebery Street were built around 1900 and the street was named after Arthur Primrose, Lord Rosebery, a prominent Liberal politician of the time who was briefly Prime Minister succeeding Gladstone. The Council was feuing land along both sides of Mid Stocket Road in the 1850s although some of the land was still available to let for grazing at this time. In 1894, the Council approved the name of Rosebery Street. By 1895 work was going ahead with the construction of homes with the Council laying gas and water mains to the properties.

Bonnymuir Place runs from Mid Stocket Road to Westburn Road and was laid out in the latter years of the 19th century on ground owned by Aberdeen University. The street was named after a parcel of land in the vicinity called Bonnymuir. In the *Aberdeen Journal* of Wednesday, December 31st, 1823, the Cottage of Bonnymuir was advertised to let with 3 acres of ground just 20 minutes walk from Aberdeen. Bonnymuir Cottage can be seen on Alexander Gibb's 19th century map of the area on the South Stocket Road which is now King's Gate and Beechgrove Terrace. Behind the houses, in the lane on the right, lies Bonnymuir Bowling Club which was established in 1922/23 by local bowling enthusiasts.

Standing: W H Davidson, G Cooper, C B Garrioch, J S Taylor, A Craig, W Allan, C G Davidson, A Milne, J Reid, W Tocher, J M McFarlane, J Rigg, J M Ross
Sitting: J Gordon, A G R Weir, R Cameron (Treasurer), J M Begg (Vice President), G H Simpson (President), P Scott, E Swan (Secretary), H Reid, A Matthews.

In 1922, the company of Bonnymuir Bowling Green Ltd was set up with a view to establishing a green in garden area at the rear of Bonnymuir Place. A board of directors was appointed with Mr. G H Simpson as chair. The green was laid out by Messrs Provan of Glasgow and paid for by the members. By 1923, the membership stood at around 100. By October 1923, it was reported that the aim of the directors to open the green free of debt was close to fruition. A bazaar was held in the Music Hall and raised £450 towards the bowling green fund. Several other fund-raising events also added to the total. The green was a huge success in the area for many years but sadly has now had to close due to lack of support.

Albyn Place runs from Alford Place (at Holburn Junction) to Queen's Cross. In this Edwardian photograph looking west, we see two well-dressed ladies waiting for the tram to take them into town. The lamp standard carries a board indicating the tramway station or stop. The tram coming towards the ladies is heading east to Castle Street. In the distance is Queen's Cross Church, a Free Church of Scotland building constructed in 1881. There is a horse and cart beside the approaching tram showing the considerable space between the tram lines and the kerb. Thus, passengers had to step into the road to get onto the tram as can be seen here. However, with much less traffic, this was not as hazardous as it would be today. The tram going towards Queen's Cross is going to Bay View on Queen's Road. Two young school girls can be seen on the left in their uniforms with panama hats and black stockings.

Originally called the Alford Road, Albyn Place was one of the first streets to be laid out on the estate of Skene of Rubislaw. James Skene, the then owner of the estate, had a house in Albyn Place in the Georgian New Town in Edinburgh and it is thought that he named the new street after his home in the capital. Archibald Simpson was called upon to design imposing villas set back along the tree-lined street to create an impression of wealth and substance. 19 Albyn Place, the building on the left of the photograph, designed by Archibald Simpson in 1837-9, was Mrs. Elmslie's Institution. Mrs. Elmslie was a wealthy benefactor who bought a large plot of land in Albyn Place to create a home and school for orphan girls.

In 1891 the building was bought to accommodate the Aberdeen High School for Girls (previously the English School sited in Little Belmont Street). The High School expanded east into No 18 Albyn Place and west into No 20 as the school roll increased. In February 1935 there was a serious fire at the school when the school hall, laundry and cookery rooms were completely burned out. The fact that the school had no telephone led to a delay in calling the fire brigade as the janitor had to run to a garage in Albyn Lane to use their telephone. After this incident, the Grammar, Central and High Schools all had telephones installed. In 1936 a proposal to unify the three buildings was put before the Council and passed. The cost of the work was estimated at £115,000. With the additional space created, school roll increased to 1,000. The primary department was closed and the secondary school increased until it was the largest school in Aberdeen. The school became co-educational and was renamed Harlaw Academy in 1974.

In the First World War, hospital accommodation was desperately needed to care for the masses of wounded men returning from the front. The 1st Scottish General Hospital was set up. However, there was insufficient accommodation at the designated hospitals like Oldmill – now Woodend Hospital – for all the wounded. Some of whom were treated in hastily-converted schools and some even in huts and tents. The photograph shows wounded officers relaxing at Aberdeen High School for Girls which was among those requisitioned.

The school was founded by Miss Harriet Warrack in 1867 as an independent boarding school for the daughters of prosperous merchants and professional men. It started life in Union Place, as the western end of Union Street was known, and was called the Union Place Seminary for Young Ladies. Mr. Alexander Mackie joined the school and became joint head teacher with Miss Warrack. In 1886 the school had moved to 4-6 Albyn Place and was known as the Albyn Place School. Mr. Mackie was then in sole charge. In 1925 the school moved again to Queen's Road. This building is now offices.

Rubislaw Terrace stands back from Albyn Place with broad private gardens in front of this and the adjacent Queen's Terrace (built circa 1871) giving that part of Albyn place a feeling of space and grandeur. It is a terrace of fine granite homes of two storeys, basement and attic. The gardens were called an 'Ornamental Plantation' in the original feuing plan in 1848. Built on the Rubislaw estate, it was designed by Thomas Mackenzie and James Matthews. James Giles RSA, a landscape architect was also involved in the design. The terrace is listed category B. Built in the latter half of the 19th century, it reflected the affluence of wealthy Aberdonians while underlining the class divide as people of means moved westwards out of the old crowded city. Professor Matthew Hay, founder of the Aberdeen Joint Hospitals scheme and of Foresterhill Hospital, lived with his family in Rubislaw Terrace. A flight of steps leads to the elevated ground floor rooms whose windows have leaded privacy glass panels in the lower section. In 1856 one of the houses in the terrace, together with a coach house and two stalled stable was put up for sale with an estimated price of £1,000. At this time, a working man might earn £1 per week. The gardens are now open to the public and are maintained by Aberdeen City Council.

Carden Place United Free Church stands at the corner of Carden Place and Albert Street. This handsome Gothic building was designed by Robert Wilson of Ellis and Wilson in 1880. Wilson was an elder of the church. The church was opened on the 2nd April 1882 and cost £11,500. The congregation amalgamated with Melville Church (designed by Brown and Watt) which stood at the corner of Skene Street and Rose Street. It was named after the religious reformer Andrew Melville. The church then became known as Carden Melville. In 1989 Carden Melville Church amalgamated with Queen's Cross Church and the building was converted into offices.

At the junction of Carden Place and Albert Terrace lies St. Mary's Episcopal Church, better known to Aberdonians as the Tartan Kirk. It is so called because of the different colours of granite used in its construction. It was built in the 1860s to house part of the congregation of St. John's, Crown Terrace following a dispute. The building is Grade A listed by Historic Scotland. During an air raid in the Second World War, the chancel was hit by a half ton cluster bomb causing massive damage. The church was repaired by the War Damage Commission aided by generous donations. The area of damage can be identified by the granite – the repair is plain grey. Albert Terrace was built between 1848 and 1867 to a design by Archibald Simpson and is listed Grade B by Historic Scotland. The terrace has retained its cassies (granite setts) maintaining the original appearance. The houses are deceptively spacious having been constructed on sloping ground.

This is a photograph of the Grammar School. The entrance is on Skene Street at its junction with Esslemont Avenue. It has been on the present site since 1863 when it moved from Schoolhill where it had been for at least 400 years. The first record of the Grammar School is in 1418. When the school was first built in Schoolhill, it was in an open airy space with the nearest building being the St. Nicholas (the Mither Kirk). By 1863 the school interior was cramped due to increases in pupils and it was hemmed in with newer buildings, losing the feeling of space. The fees for pupils attending the old school were 10s 6d for both juniors and seniors per term. Shortly after the new school opened, the fees rose to 15s for juniors and £1 for seniors. This was a large increase for families. The present school buildings were designed by James Matthews and by Matthew & MacKenzie. Constructed of Rubislaw granite, at a cost of £13,000 from the Common Good Fund, the opening of the new buildings took place on Friday 23rd October 1863. The ceremony included prize giving from the previous academic year in the old buildings. Arguably the most famous pupil to attend the school was Lord Byron who attended in the last decade of the 18th century. A granite statue of him stands at the school entrance. A major fire in the 1980s destroyed much of the interior of the oldest part of the school. However, the external fabric of the school has been restored and the interior is now a practical, modern place of learning.